# MAHMOUD

# MAHMOUD

## BY TARA GRAMMY & TOM ARTHUR DAVIS

PLAYWRIGHTS CANADA PRESS
TORONTO

LIBRARY AND ARCHIVES CANADA CATALOGUING IN PUBLICATION
Grammy, Tara, 1988-, author
    Mahmoud / Tara Grammy and Tom Arthur Davis.

A play.
Issued in print and electronic formats.
ISBN 978-1-77091-324-0 (pbk.).--ISBN 978-1-77091-325-7 (pdf).--
ISBN 978-1-77091-326-4 (epub)

    I. Davis, Tom Arthur, 1988-, author  II. Title.

PS8613.R354M34 2015        C812'.6        C2014-908385-8
                                          C2014-908386-6

We acknowledge the financial support of the Canada Council for the Arts, the Ontario Arts Council (OAC), the Ontario Media Development Corporation, and the Government of Canada through the Canada Book Fund for our publishing activities.

For our mothers, Arta and Marlane,
who taught us to be dreamers.

For our fathers, Bob and Khosrow, who
taught us to keep our feet on the ground.

The first spark was inspired by Paul Klee's painting *Dance of the Red Skirts*. Leah Cherniak had shown us this piece in our fourth-year drama performance class at the University of Toronto as a place from which to draw images for our self-written solo projects. This painting of a city in ruins with disjointed figures strewn around it, all wearing red, took me back to Tehran, but not the Tehran that I knew. My Tehran was a city full of love, which had grown exponentially before eyes that were blind to anything but the fun and excitement of being with my family when I visited every summer. *Dance of the Red Skirts* was the Tehran my mother's generation knew. My mother saw her home divided by revolution and desecrated by war. To her, the vibrant Tehran she knew was polluted, defeated, and tired. For a split second, and for the first time, I saw the city through her eyes, and something in me shifted.

That night, the sweet man who drove me home was an Iranian Canadian engineer-cum-cab driver whose name I regretfully never learned. This man's kind demeanour and familiar accent followed me to class the next day as I walked around the Helen Gardiner Phelan Playhouse with a duct-tape moustache and Tom's coat for a few hours, and thus the character Mahmoud was born. Our conversation about the generational divide between Iranian immigrants became the basis for my ten-minute self-written solo project. The climax of *Mahmoud*, the final conversation between Mahmoud and Tara, is only a slightly edited version of that original piece.

The following summer of 2009, after I presented my solo project to my professors and peers, the Green Movement started in Iran. I opted not to visit my family in Tehran that summer and watched the events that unfolded in my country from afar. The helplessness and anxiety that flooded the lives of Iranians all over the world was tangible. As an honorary Iranian, Tom felt it too, and we decided to develop *Mahmoud* as a full-length play to deal with these emotions.

With the developmental support of Pandemic Theatre, the dramaturgical support of Soheil Parsa, and the financial support of Toronto's Iranian community, we set out to create the full-length version of *Mahmoud*. Through hours upon hours of improvisation, laughter, and tears, we finally came up with something. It was during this period that we introduced the characters of Tara and Emanuelos. It became apparent that this play would be intensely personal, so it felt right to include details of my childhood growing up in Toronto. I knew there were many little girls like me out there, who felt lost in their multinational identities, and who would eventually grow up and deal with the same issues I faced. Drawing from real and exaggerated events in my life, Tara's story wrote itself.

We also felt the need to use the play to highlight the homophobia in Iranian immigrant communities, and the desperate need to bridge the gap between their traditional beliefs and modern realities. Much to the dismay of my friends and family, I had been playing the character of a very flamboyant Spanish man named Emanuelos de Mille Boneros Testosteronos since I was fourteen. He was very superficial and mostly gave unsolicited fashion advice to everyone around him. Inspired by my mother, who loved Emanuelos and had told us many stories about her gay Iranian friends, we came up with the storyline of Emanuelos and Behnam.

The play debuted at the Tarragon Theatre Extra Space in February 2011, two years after I performed the original ten-minute version at U of T. A series of positive reviews, and the endorsement of Woody Harrelson—who became a fan of the show after seeing it completely by chance—led to sold-out houses. Once we realized the effect the play was having on audiences, we decided to develop it even further.

The final version of *Mahmoud* was developed in the months before July 2012, when we presented it at the Toronto Fringe Festival to sold-out crowds, eventually participating in the Best of Fringe series. In August 2012, we took the play to New York City for the New York International Fringe Festival. Much to our surprise, *Mahmoud* continued to reach audiences in the Big Apple, winning Overall Excellence in Solo Performance and taking part in the Encore Series, which awarded us another week of shows off-Broadway. *Mahmoud*'s New York success found its way to Los Angeles in January of 2013, and, as they say, the rest is history.

I am humbled by the success that *Mahmoud* has met wherever it has been produced. There is no experience quite like performing *Mahmoud*. Nothing gives me the same kind of release and satisfaction. The characters have become my friends, and I am grateful to have had the chance to embody them for so long. I hope they speak to the outsider inside you, and I hope that their stories cause something, however small, to shift in your point of view.

Tara Grammy
Los Angeles, December 2014

After seeing Tara perform the first incarnation of *Mahmoud*, that short ten-minute class performance, I knew that I wanted to see more. She was too captivating as this quirky Persian cab driver to leave it undeveloped.

This was in May of 2009, exactly one month before the contested elections in Iran, which subsequently reinstated conservative president Mahmoud Ahmadinejad. In protest of seemingly fraudulent electoral practices, many Iranians took to the streets in what was dubbed the Green Movement (green being the campaign colour of Mir-Hossein Mousavi, whom many declared to be the true victor). With a very young population (60% of Iran's then population of seventy-three million were under the age of thirty), there were calls for another revolution; a call for true democracy. But the protests were not met peacefully, and many young men and women were imprisoned, beaten, and killed at the hands of pro-government militia. The death of Neda Agha-Soltan, in particular, drew international attention after she was shot by a sniper during a protest, to which she was an innocent bystander. The whole tragic event was caught on camera, the video went viral, and Neda (whose name aptly means "voice" in Persian) became the face of the opposition.

Suddenly, with this tiny ten-minute school project, we were tackling some huge socio-political topics. Whether we wanted to or not. This was not our intention—not initially at least. That sounds odd given the issues we explore in the piece, such as human-rights violations in Iran, outdated immigration policies in Canada, racism against Middle Eastern immigrants, and homophobia in Iranian immigrant communities. But really, we just loved Mahmoud's character. We wanted to make a comedy, not a piece of dogma. We are just as charmed by Mahmoud, Emanuelos, and twelve-year-old Tara as our audiences are. But they have their flaws: Mahmoud's nostalgic pride, Emanuelos's obliviousness, Tara's naïveté. It is these flaws that make them human. They wear their clownish stereotypical masks to hide behind and delight their audiences, but in the end these masks fail them, leaving us with three broken individuals left to pick up the pieces of their lives.

Beyond its political leanings, *Mahmoud* is, quite simply, a story of immigration. It strikes a chord with audiences, because this is hardly a uniquely Iranian experience: feeling helpless, uprooted, and disconnected from your homeland during tumultuous times is an experience with which most immigrants across the world can relate.

Tom Arthur Davis
Toronto, December 2014

The first iteration of *Mahmoud* was performed under the guidance of Leah Cherniak as a ten-minute production at the University of Toronto's University College Drama Program in May 2009. A fifty-minute workshopped production was subsequently produced by Pandemic Theatre at the Tarragon Theatre Extraspace, Toronto, in March 2011, with the following cast and creative team:

Performer: Tara Grammy
Director: Tom Arthur Davis
Consulting director: Soheil Parsa
Sound design: Mike Conley
Stage manager: Jenna Koenig
Lighting: Linn Øyen Farley
Set and costume design: Tara Grammy and Tom Arthur Davis
Producer: Jessica Rose
Publicity: Alex Rubin

A full-length production was mounted by Pandemic Theatre in July 2012 as part of the Toronto Fringe Festival, where it was selected for Best of Fringe and the Patrons' Pick. It featured the same creative team as the fifty-minute production, but with the addition of Omar Hady as an assistant director, and Tom Arthur Davis and Jiv Parasram as producers.

The play subsequently toured to the New York International Fringe Festival in August 2012, where it won Overall Excellence in Solo Performance and was a part of the Encore Series. The play has since moved on to performances in Los Angeles and San Francisco.

# CHARACTERS

Mahmoud
Emanuelos
Tara

# PROLOGUE

*Blackout. Drum roll. Cymbal crash. Lights up. The* PERFORMER *stands behind a Persian carpet, upon which sits a chair. The* PERFORMER *silently greets the audience, raises their hand in the air, and snaps their fingers, cueing the beginning of the show. The* PERFORMER *lowers one hand forward in a* MAHMOUD *gesture, and the rest of their body follows forward onto the carpet, turning the* PERFORMER *into* MAHMOUD.

**MAHMOUD:** Hello, my friends! How are you? Nice to seeing you. Wow! Some very good lookers here tonight. If I am knowing everybody so good-looking, I would wearing something a little bit nicer—

*MAHMOUD hears a dispatch call from his taxi.*

Sorry, my friend. Taxi call me. I have to make the pickup. I be right back—

*MAHMOUD walks off the carpet, turning back into the PERFORMER. The PERFORMER turns back to the audience and places one leg on the carpet in an EMANUELOS gesture. The rest of their body follows, turning the PERFORMER into EMANUELOS.*

**EMANUELOS:** Hello, everybody! My name is Emanuelos de Mille Boneros Testosteronos. And I am the sexiest Spanish man you've ever seen. Oh my God, are you guys Persian? I can totally tell because everyone is wearing something designer! And you are smelling like the perfume counter at the Bay.

*EMANUELOS starts to walk off the carpet.*

Seriously. You wear too much perfume.

*EMANUELOS moves off the carpet, turning back into the PERFORMER. The PERFORMER looks to the audience and moves their face forward, wearing the expression of TARA. The PERFORMER then steps onto the carpet, turning into TARA. TARA moves to sit cross-legged on the chair.*

**TARA:** Hi, um, I'm Tara, and um, okay so, tomorrow's the audition for *Peter Pan*, and I really want to be Tinker Bell, and all I've ever wanted to be is a singer slash songwriter slash actress slash UN ambassador, but I'm never even going to be that because Iranian girls become doctors. Really. Hairy. Doctors.

*TARA hears her mother calling her.*

Coming!

*TARA scurries offstage.*

# SCENE 1

*MAHMOUD emerges from offstage, steps onto the carpet, and treats the chair like one would a car, putting the key into the ignition, switching gears, adjusting mirrors, etc. Then, upon noticing the audience again:*

**MAHMOUD:** Hello again, my friends! Nice to seeing you one more time. Yes yes, my friends, my name is Mahmoud, yes, and I am IRAAAAAAAANNNNIIIIAAAANNNN! You are knowing Iran? Not IRAQ! Don't listen what they are telling you on this CNN, BBC, NBC, CBC, whatever! Iran is the land of the kings. It is the land of the emperors. It is the birthplace of civilization. It is the home of—

*MAHMOUD's cellphone rings.*

Sorry, my friends, it is my wife. You are minding I answer?

*He answers the phone.*

Alo? Salam ghorbunet berram, chashm azizam, bashe bashe, chashm chashm, ghorbunet berram, faddat sham khodafes. She is calling five hundred times a day! Where I was? Oh yes, my friends, IRAN! My friends, Iran is a very rich country. Yes yes, especially in the culture. You are knowing who Hafez is? No problem, I am keeping his book in my pocket at all times.

*He pulls out a book of poetry.*

My friends, Hafez is a poet. Best poet in the world. He is the man who is teaching the world how to love. He is teaching the world how to live! My friends, Iran is also rich in the gold and diamonds. You are knowing the Daria-i-Noor diamond? Sea-of-light diamond? No problem, no problem, I am having a picture in my pocket at all times.

*He pulls out a picture of the Daria-i-Noor diamond.*

My friends, the Daria-i-Noor diamond is the biggest diamond in all of the Asia. It is a very important—

*A taxi dispatch call.*

Sorry, my friends, I have to make the pickup. No problem, no problem.

MAHMOUD *begins to back up his cab.*

I come back, I tell you about Daria-i-Noor; I tell you about Iran, anything you are liking, my friend—

> *A loud crash.* MAHMOUD *lurches forward as though in a traffic accident.*

Canadian drivers!

> MAHMOUD *gets out of his cab and moves upstage quickly.*

What you are doing to my car?!

> MAHMOUD *motions to his car, then snaps his fingers and turns back around as* EMANUELOS.

# SCENE 2

EMANUELOS *struts downstage like a runway model,*
*offering cologne-soaked blotters to the audience. The*
*music fades out and we hear the sounds from inside*
*Holt Renfrew.*

**EMANUELOS:** *(as if to passersby)* Dolce Gabbana: The One?
Dolce Gabbana: The One? Dolce Gabbana: The One?

*He notices the audience.*

Oh, hello everybody! *(offering blotters to audience)* Dolce
Gabbana: The One?! You know what? It's almost my break,
I'm gonna take it early to talk to you. *(sitting down)* Okay, so. . .
I love this cologne so much. You wanna know why? Okay, I tell
you. I'm gay, and I am in love with the most beautiful Iranian
man you have ever seen. And this is his cologne! His name
is Behnam. Do you know him? Behhnaaam? Ah! Everybody,
let's say it together; say it with me: BEH-NAM. AH! Isn't that a

beautiful name? And do you know what it means?! It means beautiful name! ISN'T THAT PERFECT! And, oh my God, he is so perfect. The first time I am seeing him he is wearing a Tom Ford suit, with Gucci loafers, a Marc Jacobs shirt, and a perfectly folded paisley pañuelo in his suit pocket. And then he is turning to me and he is saying, "Where did you get that limited-edition Hermès satchel? I've had my name on a waiting list for years." AND THEN, the barista is handing him his Grande half fat, no foam vanilla chai latte in a Venti cup, and I know we are going to be together forever. And we were! For two years now. We're even getting married! But then his grandfather died and he is going to Iran and I have not heard from him in one week! I am so worried about him! I'm calling; I'm texting; I'm emailing; Facebook Messenger; MSN Messenger; Yahoo Messenger—any type of technology I can even think about, and I have not heard from my beautiful baby. What if something happen to him?

*EMANUELOS smells the cologne sample in his hand.*

*(as if to passersby)* But the show must go on. Dolce Gabbana: The One? Dolce Gabbana: The One? Dolce Gabbana: The One? Sir? Sir! Here. Take the whole bottle. Sir?!

*EMANUELOS moves off of the carpet, chasing the passerby offstage.*

# SCENE 3

*Inside* TARA's *middle school. A bell rings and kids run in the halls, talking.* TARA *enters wearing her backpack, skipping.*

**TARA:** *(noticing the audience)* Oh! Hey, um, so, I'm kind of late for class, but I really need to ask you guys something. Okay. Do. I. Have... Sideburns?

*TARA whips her head to the side to display her "sideburns."*

I need you to look very closely! Because I am like the rainforest that nobody wants to save! I should just move to Brazil, because I think that's where the rainforest is, and then all the boys won't go *(cough)* HAIRBALL *(cough)* HAIRBALL every time I walk into a room... But it won't be that way for long. Wanna know a secret? Okay, I'm gonna tell you but you can't tell anyone, because if my mom finds out she'll kill me. Like she'll actually like murder me like to death. Okay. With my allowance, I bought...

Two bottles of Nair hair-removal cream. AND. One bottle of Garnier number 110 extra-light BLOND hair dye!! so. Next week, when my mom is on her business trip to Jamaica, I am going to remove all the hair on my body, and dye my hair blond, and be the beautiful blond bombshell I've always felt like on the inside. Wanna know the real reason I'm doing it? Okay, so next week is the school dance, and, well, like there's this guy Joe. And I hate him. But last dance we danced together. And it. Was. Magical.

> *We shift to a school dance, which cues TARA to slow dance with an imaginary Joe.*

He's so tall. And handsome. And he's a really good basketball player, like Allen Iverson. And he's really sexy. Just like David Hasselhoff. . . but minus all the body hair.

> *The music cuts out.*

But he's in love with Nicole Lambs. Star athlete of Rose Valley Middle School, and the bane of my existence! So. I am going to show up to the dance, blond and hairless and beautiful. AND starring in *Peter Pan* as Tinker Bell. And Joe is going to fall madly in love with me and forget all about Nicole Lambs!

*We're at the school dance again.* TARA, *slow-dancing with Joe, leans in for a kiss. The school bell rings. The lights return to normal.*

I'm late!

*TARA runs offstage.*

# SCENE 4

*The sound of a microwave replaces that of the school bell. We're now in a break room.* MAHMOUD *enters eating Salad Shirazi out of a Tupperware container and reading a book of Hafez poems. He notices the audience.*

MAHMOUD: Ah, my friends! I didn't think you would being here. I am on my break. I have no food to giving you. Here. This is a little Salad Shirazi my wife she is making. Very delicious!

*MAHMOUD hands the salad to an audience member.*

Where I was before? Oh yes, my friends: Iran! My friends, Iran is the land of the kings. It is the land of the emperors. It is the birthplace of the civilization. It is the home of—

*MAHMOUD's phone rings.*

Sorry, my friends. My wife. *(into the phone)* Allo, salam ghorbunet berram, chashm azizam, bashe bashe, chashm chashm, morgham mikharam, bashe azizam, ghorbunet berram faddat sham, khodafes. *(to the audience)* Five hundred times a day! Where I was? Oh yes, my friends. The Daria-i-Noor diamond!

> MAHMOUD *reaches into his pocket for the picture, but then his face freezes. Instead he pulls out a picture of his wife, Marjan. He becomes transfixed by the photo and an azan call to prayer can be heard in the distance. It is as though he is in a dream world.* MAHMOUD *then comes back to reality as the azan fades out.*

Sorry, my friends! You know, sometimes I'm having the nightmares in the daytime. My wife, she is replacing the Daria-i-Noor picture with our wedding picture.

> *He shows the picture of Marjan to the audience.*

You want to hearing a story about my wife? Let me I tell you a little story, you know. When I was a young man, don't look at me today! Once upon a time I was very sexy! Really! Like Gregory Peck! Really! Anyway, every day my mother is saying to me, "Mahmoud, go buying the bread." And I am saying, "No, I am too cool and sexy to go buying the bread!" But after I finish the university, my father, he is buying me a Toyota Corolla!

> *He looks for a positive response from the audience.*

Toyota Corolla! Very nice car, those days. Like Mercedes-Benz! Toyota Corolla!

*He's surprised by the lack of response from the audience.*

Really? Okay. Anyway, after I am getting the car, my mother, she say to me, "Mahmoud, you are having the car, go buying the bread." So I am saying, "Okay, old woman, I go buying the bread." I go to the bakery, I walk in, and I am seeing a WOMAN. Black hair. Black eyes. Red *minijupe*. Very beautiful, you know— *(indicating big breasts)* And I am saying, "Hello. My name is Mahmoud." She is taking one look at me, one look at my car. We are married one week later! My beautiful wife Marjan, still to this day!

*The microwave beeps.*

Oh, here is the food she is making. No problem, no problem. I am coming back; I tell you all about Iran; I tell you about Marjan, anything you are wanting—

*Blackout.*

# SCENE 5

*A news reporter can be heard in reference to the "Neda" video from the 2009 elections in Iran. The lights come up on EMANUELOS watching television in horror. His phone rings.*

EMANUELOS: *(answering the phone)* Hello? Oh my God, baby! Where have you been?! I have been so worried about you! Are you okay? Oh. Oh, yeah, you told me. Oh no, I forgot. Okay! Relax! Just delete the emails. Have you been thinking about me at least? I been thinking about you! Oh my God, yesterday we went to the movies and the trailer came on for that *Prince of Persia* movie and the first time they are showing Jake Gyllenhaal and he is looking all Middle Eastern and sweaty, I thought about you. Do you thinking about me? OH! I guess there are gays in Iran! But, baby, listen, I'm hearing some really bad things coming from there. No, I know he is winning, but they are even arresting his nephew. Oh-kay! Oh-kay! Just don't go to the protest, okay? What?! Are you crazy! Did you not see that video with that girl?! Behnam, of course I worry about you! I'm calm, Behnam. I'M CALM! How's your mama? You telling her about me? Did she like the pictures I am sending? Listen, tell your father I think we should have the wedding in Toronto. I don't think I should come to Tehran. What?!

EMANUELOS *gets up and starts to walk offstage.*

But we're only talking for two minutes! Okay, baby, okay, I love you. Asheghettam. Khodafes. I'm like the Spanish shah!

EMANUELOS *laughs as he exits.*

# SCENE 6

*TARA enters, running across upstage from wing to wing. She does this several times, finally re-entering holding her headshot and stepping onto the carpet. She then walks to an audience member and hands them her photo.*

**TARA:** This is my headshot. I know you didn't ask for one, but I'm very professional. I'm Tara, from 6B, Miss Wakabayashi's class, and I'm auditioning for the part of Tinker Bell. I wrote the song myself, music as well as lyrics, and I choreographed the dance as well, so please feel free to write triple or quadruple threat on your sheet. And I am ready to begin.

*TARA turns her back to the audience. She then quickly turns around, singing and dancing in a very dramatic fashion, boy-band style.*

*(singing)* Stop with all these games
You're drivin' me insane

Now you're back again
And you want more
Of all these games
You're puttin' me through so much pain
You're back again and you want more.

> *She finishes with a point out to the audience and bows with an exuberant smile. Upon coming up from her bow, her smile turns into a frown and she collapses to the ground.*

I need. Some Backstreet Boys!

> *"Show Me the Meaning of Being Lonely" by the Backstreet Boys plays.*

I always dreamed I'd be the sixth member of the Backstreet Boys. Like an honorary female member. Nick would see me in the audience, and he'd take my hand, and he'd pull me up on stage, and give me a microphone, and I would be too talented and beautiful for him not to make me the sixth member of the Backstreet Boys. But that'll never happen to me.

> *The song cuts out.*

To Nicole Lambs maybe. Star athlete of Rose Valley Middle School, and now starring in *Peter Pan* as Tinker Bell! She sang "Somewhere Over the Rainbow." ORIGINAL! And she didn't even get the lyrics right. How hard can it be? *(singing)* "Somewhere over the rainbow. . . what-e-ver!" Whatever. I am going to show up to the dance, blond and hairless and beautiful, and Joe is still going to fall madly in love with me and I am still going to WIN over NICOLE LAMBS!

   *Suddenly a car can be heard driving and splashing through a large puddle.*

# SCENE 7

*After the splash, we are back on the streets of Toronto. TARA turns into MAHMOUD, who has just been hit with the wave of water.*

**MAHMOUD:** Watch where you are going, you bastard!

*MAHMOUD notices the audience.*

Oh! Sorry, my friends. Normally I am a nice man, but today. Today is not a good day.

*He gets into his cab.*

And it is very hot in here.

*He opens the car window and spits out of it.*

Young girl. She is getting into my cab today. Nice-looking girl; pretty little girl, you know, and she is crying! Looking so sad, saying something about Tinkerbox. She is looking a little Iranian, so I am trying to making her feel better. I am saying to her, "My girl, are you IRAAANNIAAANN?" And she is saying, "NO! I am Iranian Canadian!" What you are meaning you are Iranian Canadian?! Iran is having a five-thousand-year history!

*He pulls out his Hafez book.*

We are the home of Hafez, Rumi, Saadi, Ferdowsi, my friends! Best poets in the world! What is Canada the home of, huh? HUH? CELINE DION? Canada is having two-hundred-year history. My grandmother is two hundred years old! IRANIAN CANADIAN?!

*In a fit of rage MAHMOUD throws the book out of the window.*

*(realizing he has thrown his book)* Ay Ba Ba!

*MAHMOUD gets out of the car and steps off the carpet. Upon so doing he transforms back into the PERFORMER, who gives a quick look to the audience and quickly walks offstage.*

# SCENE 8

*TARA enters wearing a ridiculous blond wig. The school dance music plays. TARA stands at the edge of the carpet, checking herself out in an imaginary mirror. She's pretty enamoured with her new hair. She steps forward onto the carpet. The music cuts out and TARA's mood completely changes.*

**TARA:** So. When God closes a window, he opens a door, eh? WELL NOT MY GOD. My God closed ALL the windows, and then bolted the door shut, so that I would be stuck in this empty room of misery and sadness for the rest of eternity! Unless I break open one of those windows, and throw myself out, and be reborn as a brand-new baby. And y'know what I'd do? I would choose to be from somewhere normal! Like Hamilton. And I'd choose to have normal parents who give me peanut butter and jelly sandwiches for lunch instead of Ghormeh sabzi, which makes me smell ethnic ALL DAY! But you know what I would choose most of all? I would choose to be born in a regular human body instead of one that originally belonged to a GORILLA!

*TARA throws her blond wig into the audience.*

Sorry. So I went to the dance. And I looked darn good! And I walked right up to Joe, and I said, "Oh, hey Joe." And he said, "Tara?! Is that you? What'd you do to your hair?" I looked so good that he didn't even recognize me! "Oh, nothing. I was lying in the sun and it lightened a bit. So I just dyed the rest of it to match." "Yeah, looks good. Listen, can I ask you something?" "Yeah, sure, whatever." "Um, can you come here for a sec?" That's when I leaned in and I could smell his manly deodorant, and that's when he was supposed to ask me to dance with him, and then we were supposed to kiss, and then get married, and have babies, and move to a castle in Switzerland. But that's not what happened. "Will you ask Nicole if she'll dance with me? She's like right there but I'm like way too nervous to talk to her." "Yeah. . . sure. . ."

*TARA runs offstage, shattered and crying.*

# SCENE 9

*MAHMOUD enters searching for the Hafez book he threw out the window. He finally finds it and picks it up.*

**MAHMOUD:** Oh, my friends. Crazy man—foolish man to throw Hafez out the window!

*MAHMOUD gets back into his cab.*

In my culture Hafez is like a holy book. Whenever you are having a problem in your life, a question, something bothering you, you know, you are opening his pages and he is always giving you the best answer. This book was given to me by my favourite professor at the university. You are knowing I am engineer? Yes, yes, my friends. I am engineer! Top risk. VIP! My friends, I am telling you so much about Iran, about Marjan, I forget to tell you about the most important thing... MAHMOUD! Yes, yes. You know, when I am first coming to Canada, it is very difficult. After the war. Have to be smuggled out of Iran. Lots of problems. Twenty-five year later and I am still having the nightmares, but no problem, no problem. I think I am coming here; tomorrow I am getting the job. Everywhere I am going they are saying you are not having the right qualification. What you are meaning I don't having the right qualification?! After one year I am getting very angry, getting very frustrated, you know. One day I am coming home and my wife, she is saying to me, "Mahmoud, our next-door neighbour, he is Pakistani, doctor, and he is driving taxi. Why you don't driving taxi?" "What you are meaning, I drive taxi?! I have a Ph.D. in electrical engineering! I work for best engineering firm in Tehran! I am the reason Tehran is even having electricity! What you are meaning I am driving the taxi! No one will respect me!" "But, Mahmoud, we are needing the money." "What you are meaning we are needing the money?! I am having the biggest house in the best neighbourhood in Tehran! I am having house in the north, villa in the south! Cars, servants, whatever I am wanting! What you are meaning I drive taxi? We are needing the money?!" . . . But I am looking at her, you know, and I am seeing she is missing our life in Iran too. But she is a good woman, a kind woman, and she is saying to me, "Mahmoud. . . maybe they are having the Toyota Corolla."

*Silence.* MAHMOUD *regrettably gives in.*

"Okay, woman, I am driving taxi." Twenty-five years later, I am still engineer of my taxi! And I am knowing the streets of Toronto better than my wife Marjan is knowing her famous recipe for fesenjoon.

MAHMOUD *starts to change the radio station, flipping through static. Finally he lands on "Conga" by Miami Sound Machine. He starts to dance a typical old-man Iranian dance. During a peak in the music, he raises his arm over his head and snaps his fingers, turning into* EMANUELOS.

# SCENE 10

*EMANUELOS gets up and dances to the music, rumba style. He then moves toward the audience.*

**EMANUELOS:** Hello, everbody— Oh my God! Is that Gloria Estefan? Who can stay sitting to Gloria Estefan?! Okay! *(to audience)* Who has a camera phone? Anybody? Somebody must have a camera phone. And I know you didn't turn it off! You? Okay. I need you to film me. When you're done, I need you to send it to behnamissexy@yahoo.ca. Okay! Ready? Okay.

*EMANUELOS dances lavishly, improvising with the audience: "Get my booty! Watch this! You like that move?"*

*EMANUELOS's phone rings.*

Hold on, oh no, I'm so sorry! Pause it, pause it! Stop the music!

*The music stops. He answers the phone.*

Hello? Hi, baby! How are you? Oh nothing, I'm just making you a little present! I've got Santa's little helpers helping me. How are you? Where are you? Oh really? Oh, that's good! What? Who's that? Behnam? Behnam?! Don't do that! I don't like it when you do that, Behnam!

*He hangs up the phone.*

Uh! He is always doing that lately! Every time I am talking to him, at first he's all sweet and sexy, but then I hear somebody coming in the room and he pretends like I'm his stockbroker! Stockbroker?! Is he embarrassed of me? Would a stockbroker do this?

*EMANUELOS snaps his fingers and the music plays. He dances in his chair. He quickly snaps his fingers again, stopping the music.*

You know what, I'm going to take that video *(points to the person in the audience who took the video)* and send it to his mama and papa. Then we'll show him what a stockbroker looks like! Play the music!

*EMANUELOS throws his hand in the air as to start dancing again. He turns into TARA raising her hand in a classroom.*

# SCENE 11

*The school bell rings.*

**TARA:** I'll go! I'll go!

*TARA gets up and stands in front of the audience as though they are in a drama class.*

This monologue is Juliet's DEATH monologue from *Romeo and Juliet* by William Shakespeare. I'll be playing Juliet.

Farewell! God knows when we shall meet again.
I have a faint cold fear thrills through my veins,
That almost freezes up the heat of life:
I'll call them back again to comfort me:
Nurse! What should she do here?
My dismal scene I needs must act alone.
Come, vial.
What if this mixture do not work at all?

Shall I be married then tomorrow morning?
No, no: this shall forbid it! . . . It's a dagger.
Lie thou there.

> TARA *mimes sticking the dagger into her stomach. She*
> *dies very dramatically, falling to the floor.* TARA *gets*
> *up quickly and bows. She snaps her fingers. She is older*
> *now, in her mid twenties. She speaks frankly to the*
> *audience.*

Well. It was in this moment I decided I was just going to be who
I was. And who I was, beneath all that hair, was an actor. But
living in a place like Toronto where your ethnicity is your mon-
ey-maker, I found it hard to be seen as anything but Iranian. So
I dyed my hair blond, properly this time, and I thought I looked
pretty neutral, and I managed to score a meeting with one of
the top agents in all of Toronto, who's opening line to me was,
"so. . . what are you. . . Arab?" Promising. "No, actually, I'm
Iranian." "That's what I said. Listen! I'm one of the top agents
in LA? Yeah, that's right, not just Toronto, but Los-fuckin'-
Angeles. You know why? Because I'm the best there fuckin'
is, that's why!" Charming. "Get up! Turn around. Good body.
Good face. Can you act?" No, I just came here to humiliate and
dehumanize myself. "Good. Look, you're gonna have to dye
your hair black. I can't sell you with that blond hair. I've gotta
sell you for all the new stuff happening. You know, that sexy
foreign vixen stuff. That girl next door *terrorist* stuff. Actually,
here's a picture of your competition." He handed me the picture
of an Indian girl. "Listen, come back to me when you've dyed

your hair black, throw on some tighter jeans, and maybe take a couple acting classes."

*TARA gets up and leaves, deflated.*

# SCENE 12

*The sounds of the streets.* EMANUELOS *runs out, hailing a cab.*

**EMANUELOS:** TAXI! TAXI!

*EMANUELOS gets into the cab.*

HI! I'm going to Holt Renfrew. It's just a few blocks from here.

**MAHMOUD:** No problem, no problem. I am taking you!

**EMANUELOS:** *(making small talk)* So, nice day today. . .

*(his phone rings)* Hello? Hi, baby! How are you? How was your flight? Okay. Okay, you call me later. I love you. Asheghettam! Khodafes! *(hangs up)*

**MAHMOUD:** *(raising an eyebrow)* Are you speaking Persian?

**EMANUELOS:** Yes, but I only know a few words. I can say *Salam*, *Khodafes*, *Chetori*, *Asheghettam*, and *Ghormeh sabzi*.

**MAHMOUD:** Wow! Where you are learning such beautiful Persian words?

**EMANUELOS:** Oh, my boyfriend's Iranian!

**MAHMOUD:** *(horrified)* Your boyfriend?

**EMANUELOS:** Yes, just like you! Oh my God! You should teach me how to say something!

**MAHMOUD:** Ah, I don't think—

**EMANUELOS:** OKAY! Teach me how to say "I love you very very much."

**MAHMOUD:** Sir, I don't think this is—

**EMANUELOS:** OKAY! Teach me how to say "your eyes are as blue as the ocean."

**MAHMOUD:** Sir, I am not comfortable with—

**EMANUELOS:** OKAY OKAY OKAY! Teach me how to say, oh this is a good one, "Your butt looks so sexy in those jeans."

**MAHMOUD:** ENOUGH!

*MAHMOUD stops the car, screeching the brakes.*

Get out.

**EMANUELOS:** But, we're not even there yet.

**MAHMOUD:** Sir, I don't want any trouble, just get out.

**EMANUELOS:** Okay. RACIST!

*EMANUELOS gets out of the cab, slamming the door behind him. MAHMOUD waits for him to exit.*

**MAHMOUD:** Sorry, my friends. Normally, I am a very nice man, but these people—

*MAHMOUD's phone rings. He goes to answer.*

I telling you, five hundred times a day. Oh! My friends, it is actually my nephew; he is in Iran. You are minding I answer?

*He answers the phone.*

Salam BEHNAM jan. How are you, *Amoo*? Nice to hearing your voice; we are already missing you here. Behnam *jan*, I spoke to your father this morning. I am hearing you are liking the *girl* we are choosing for you. Very good, very good. Behnam *jan*, listen to me, it is time you are getting married. You bring her here, she cook for you, she clean for you, you are making the babies. Enough of this dancing around you are doing, Behnam *jan*. Do you love her? What you are meaning you don't know her! She is beautiful, she is coming from good family, what more do you needing for love?! Okay, okay. I talk to you later. One last thing, *Amoo*. Make your family proud!

*An intercom pages someone inside Holt Renfrew, and* MAHMOUD *becomes* EMANUELOS.

## SCENE 13

*EMANUELOS texts on his phone at work. He is clearly upset from his cab ride.*

**EMANUELOS:** Okay. Okay! I'm working. Relax!

*EMANUELOS gets up reluctantly and starts to half-heartedly offer cologne samples to passersby.*

Dolce Gabbana: The One? Dolce Gabbana: The One? Dolce Gabbana: The One?

**TARA:** Thanks.

**EMANUELOS:** You're pretty.

**TARA:** Thank you.

**EMANUELOS:** Such big eyes.

**TARA:** Yeah, well, I'm Iranian. We're kinda known for the big eyes.

**EMANUELOS:** *(challenging)* Oh! You're Iranian. My boyfriend's Iranian!

**TARA:** That's awesome.

**EMANUELOS:** *(surprised)* Oh. . . His name is Behnam Tehrani. Do you know him?

**TARA:** We don't actually all know each other.

**EMANUELOS:** Oh. I'm missing him so much. He is in Iran right now.

**TARA:** Oh really? Just to visit?

**EMANUELOS:** No. His grandfather died.

**TARA:** Oh my God. I'm so sorry.

**EMANUELOS:** It's okay. He was ready to die like a hundred years ago. You wanna know the real reason why he's going? He's actually going to tell his family about me. We're getting married!

**TARA:** Married. To an Iranian guy? Wow. He must come from a really open-minded family.

**EMANUELOS:** No. He is always saying they are very traditional.

**TARA:** That's weird. . .

**EMANUELOS:** *(challenging)* Why?!

**TARA:** I. I don't know. . .

**EMANUELOS:** Well if you don't know, then you don't talk, okay!

**TARA:** . . .Okay. Oh! So he's going to be there for the elections. That's great. I really wish I could be there!

**EMANUELOS:** Yeah. He's really excited to vote!

*Blackout.*

## SCENE 14

*The "Neda" video can be heard in the background: people screaming, chaos.* TARA *is seen sitting on the chair, watching television in terror. She watches for a few moments before her phone rings. She scrambles to answer it. The television noises slowly fade out.*

**TARA:** Hello? Hi, Mommy? Did you talk to him? What? Oh my God! Are you sure? Oh my God! No, all the lines are cut; I can't call him. I can't relax right now, Mom! Alan aabo aroom shoddan saram nemishe! Can you call my grandparents? Okay. Call me back.

> TARA *hangs up the phone and sits again, anxious. A long silence. Finally, her phone rings again.*

Hello? Hello?

*She hears only static, a poor connection.*

*(relieved, but worried)* Daddy? Hello? Daddy?!

*The static rapidly increases in volume.*

What?! I can't hear you. Hello?! You're breaking up. Allo?!

*The static reaches its highest volume and then cuts out with a blackout.*

# SCENE 15

*During the blackout the beeping of a heart monitor in a hospital can be heard. The lights come back up on* MAHMOUD *sleeping in his cab. As he sleeps, the sounds of the azān, a crying baby, and the beeping are heard. He is having his nightmare. Suddenly his alarm goes off and he wakes up. Clearly distraught, he takes out his Hafez book and starts to read.*

**MAHMOUD:** *(from "Song of Spring")* Nafaseh bade saba mosh-kfeshan khahad shod. Aalame peer degar bare javan khahad shod. Arghavan jaame aghighi be sanam khahad dad, cheshme narges be shaghayegh negaran khadad shod.

*MAHMOUD's phone rings. He takes it out, smiles, and then goes to answer it. As he does, he turns into* EMANUELOS *talking to Behnam on the phone.*

# SCENE 16

**EMANUELOS:** Baby?! Oh my God, can you believe I get to see you in twenty-four hours?! I can't wait to kiss your pretty lips. How are you? Where are you? Baby, I have to tell you something. I bought like seventeen bottles of Dom Pérignon. I know, it's crazy, but I can't wait to see you! And to celebrate! Behnam? Baby? Don't joke with me right now, I'm too excited. This isn't funny, Behnam. Behnam? Why are you crying?

*EMANUELOS stands up in shock.*

What? They can't make you do this, Behnam. They can't make you do anything. You're only lying to yourself. This isn't fair. Behnam, this isn't fair.

*EMANUELOS pauses.*

You're a coward.

EMANUELOS *hangs up the phone and stands still and silent. After a moment his phone begins to ring again.* EMANUELOS *ignores the phone and defiantly walks off the carpet. Upon doing so, he turns into* TARA, *who is standing in the streets of Toronto.*

# SCENE 17

**TARA:** *(on the phone)* Yeah. Yeah, I'm on my way now. Just about to hop into a cab. Okay. Bye.

*TARA hangs up and hails a taxi.*

TAXI!

*TARA gets into the car.*

Hi. Sorry, I'm not going very far, and I hate to take cabs and not go very far, but I'm really really late.

**MAHMOUD:** No problem, no problem. I am taking you. Where you are going?

**TARA:** Uh, Hart House. It's at U of T. King's College Circle.

**MAHMOUD:** Yes, yes, of course. University of Toronto. Very nice, very nice. You are a student?

**TARA:** Yes, actually. I'm a theatre student.

**MAHMOUD:** Theatre? University of Toronto? *(doubtingly)* Very nice, very nice. I, myself, I am engineer. Yes, yes. Top risk. VIP.

**TARA:** That's awesome.

*An awkward silence.* TARA *notices his taxi licence.*

Hey. Your name is Mahmoud. My uncle's name is Mahmoud. You must be Iranian. I'm Iranian too.

**MAHMOUD:** Bah bah bah! An Iranian girl! But you don't looking Iranian. Why you make the hair blond? Iranian woman's beauty is in her black eyes and black hair.

**TARA:** Man farisimam kheili khube, mitunim ba ham farsi harf bezanim.

**MAHMOUD:** My girl, it is my dream to speaking Farsi with you! But my wife is calling five hundred times a day; she is saying, Mahmoud don't speaking Farsi. Practise your English; you are having accent. I live here twenty-five years, you are thinking I am having accent?

**TARA:** *(after a pause)* No.

**MAHMOUD:** So you have been back to Iran?

**TARA:** Oh yeah, I go back all the time. My family lives there so. . .

**MAHMOUD:** I haven't seen my family in twenty-five years! But is okay, you know; my wife, she is here; my nephew, he is here; the rest of them, I speak to on telephone.

**TARA:** Twenty-five years! That's older than me! Forget about your family, don't you miss the food? Kabab, Del o Jigar? Goje Sabz?

**MAHMOUD:** I have not eaten food in twenty-five years! Believe me, the food here is having no taste.

**TARA:** And the air. There's just something in the air. I'm from Tehran, which is really polluted, so there's definitely something in the air. But my dad, he takes me up to the mountains at night, and when you get out of the car and you breathe in it's like you're really breathing in oxygen. And then you look up and the stars. . . they changed my life.

**MAHMOUD:** I am liking you. You are smart girl. I tell you, I missing Iran every minute. Every smell, every taste, my family, my friends, the street where I am growing up, there is my home, you know? People here thinking I am Arab. Want to make jihad. It's funny, but. . . You know they are saying that time is making you forget? I can only remember.

**TARA:** Can I ask you something? If you miss Iran so much, and you are an engineer, why are you here? Why don't you go back?

**MAHMOUD:** It is more difficult to understand. Once upon a time I was engineer, now I am engineer of my taxi. Why you don't go back?

**TARA:** You know, I've been thinking about it a lot lately. There's nothing really keeping me here.

**MAHMOUD:** There is freedom here.

**TARA:** Yeah, okay, there's freedom, but at what cost? Being alone? Being mistreated? Everyone here ends up being some sort of slave, a servant to the system.

**MAHMOUD:** Servant?! I am not a servant. I am driving taxi because I like it! Forget about Iran. Where you are going, this is not Iran. It is a garbage can!

**TARA:** How can you just turn your back on it like that? You could be doing things in Iran, helping Iran. Your education is being wasted in this cab.

**MAHMOUD:** You are grown up here with your easy life. You are lucky! What pain you are seeing? What hardship you are seeing? Be grateful! Listen to me. Your blood is Iranian, but my soul is Iranian.

**TARA:** That's not fair! It wasn't always easy for me growing up here. I didn't choose to come here. It was a choice that was made for me. Do you know how long it took me to come to. . . you know what? This isn't a competition. All I am saying is that it is a disgrace for an Iranian engineer to drive a cab in Toronto. And by the way, I'm on my way to a protest right now. Whose soul is more Iranian?

**MAHMOUD:** My whole life is a protest! Who do you think is throwing out the old government and look where it is taking us? It was my generation who originate the revolution! Look what it is doing to us! You want what happened to us to happen to you? You have never even seen the real Iran!

**TARA:** This "real Iran" your generation keeps talking about doesn't exist anymore. It's changed! And you either need to change with it, or fight to change it!

> MAHMOUD *pulls over the cab and puts it in park. An azān call to prayer mixed with contemporary music can be heard playing softly in the background. It begins to escalate in volume throughout the following monologue.*

**MAHMOUD:** You want to hear a story about the real Iran, little girl?! I tell you a story about the really, really real Iran! One day I buy my wife, my Marjan, a sunglasses. Red colour. She is eight-month pregnant with our first baby and the colour red looking beautiful on her. But is after revolution, she cannot wearing her red *minijupe*, so we are changing with the times. I am buying her a red sunglasses instead. She is going out to buy some bread from the bakery. She is gone ten minutes, one hour, two hours. I am getting worried. So I go to the bakery. "Where is my wife?" "They are taking her." "What you are meaning? Who is taking her!" So I run to the headquarters. "Where is my wife?! Where is my wife?!" Nobody answers me. They send me to this room, that room. Two hours, finally some bastard is saying she is in the hospital. "Hospital?!" So I am running to the hospital. "What happened?!" Some bastard is asking her, "Why you are wearing those sunglasses?" And she is saying, "Because of the sun." And they are pushing her. They are pushing her so hard she is falling into the gutter, and it is killing the baby. You go back there? They kill my baby. They almost kill my wife because she is wearing red sunglasses. And I can't even say something! I say something they do it to my brother; they do it to my mother; they do it to my sister. You go back there? They are turning your whole world black, and you can't even say something. I am still having the nightmares twenty-five years later! We are having no voice—

*MAHMOUD covers his mouth with his hands. The azān prayer spikes in volume, drowning out the rest of the scene, but it continues as MAHMOUD and TARA argue, silently. After some time, MAHMOUD's voice returns for one final line.*

I am still having the nightmares!

*Percussion is added to the azān, suddenly causing the PERFORMER to re-enact MAHMOUD's nightmare.*

*The nightmare involves the repetition of four gestures:*

*A reaching out.*

*Getting struck in the side.*

*Getting struck in the back.*

*A half fall to the ground.*

*At some point the PERFORMER begins to dance, removing their jacket and raising it above their head in defiance and joy. But once the jacket is raised, the movements continue more violently. As the repetitions reach their climax, the PERFORMER stops and slowly places their hands on their stomach. The PERFORMER is then struck one final time, bringing them to the ground. They remain motionless.*

*As the lights fade to black, the PERFORMER slowly raises up off the ground and stands before the audience.*

*Silence. Blackout.*

*The azān prayer slowly fades out.*

*The end.*

Tara Grammy is an Iranian Canadian actor and playwright. She was born in Tehran, but grew up in Toronto, with a few years spent in the United States and Germany. Tara currently lives in Los Angeles but travels to Toronto often.

Tom Arthur Davis is a playwright, actor, producer, and director. He is the artistic director of Pandemic Theatre, a Toronto-based theatre company with a mandate for socio-political work. He is also a core member of the Wrecking Ball, a political performance cabaret.

First edition: February 2015
Printed and bound in Canada by Imprimerie Gauvin, Gatineau

Cover art and design by Patrick Gray

**PLAYWRIGHTS
CANADA PRESS**

202-269 Richmond St. W.
Toronto, ON
M5V 1X1

416.703.0013
info@playwrightscanada.com
playwrightscanada.com

MIX
Paper from
responsible sources
FSC® C100212